The Shoppii

Mrs. Jones opened the fridge and looked inside. There was only one small piece of cheese left. So she sat down and wrote "cheese" on a shopping list.

Ben came home from school.
He saw the shopping list
and smiled.

He picked up a pen
and wrote "chocolates"
and "raspberries"
on the list.

When Maria came home, she read the shopping list. She saw that Ben had put some special treats on it.

Shopping List
cheese
chocolates
raspberries

So Maria picked up
the pen and put
"ice cream" and "nuts"
on the shopping list.
She liked ice cream
with chopped nuts.

Shopping List
cheese
chocolates
raspberries
ice cream
nuts

Soon Mr. Jones came home.
He read the shopping list
and smiled.

He loved all the treats
on the list. But the thing
he liked best was not on it.

Mr. Jones poured
himself a glass of juice.
Then he picked up the pen
and added "juice" to
the shopping list.

Just then, Ben and Maria came inside. They had been playing with Jed, their dog.

Jed was excited to see Mr. Jones. He ran inside and raced up to him.

Oh no! Jed bumped into the table. The glass of juice tipped over onto the shopping list.

Mrs. Jones came into the kitchen to see what all the fuss was about. Mr. Jones was holding the wet shopping list.

18

Mrs. Jones took the list and looked at it.
"We'd better go to the supermarket while we can still read the list," she said.

"Will we buy chocolates
and raspberries?"
asked Ben.

"Will we buy
ice cream and nuts?"
asked Maria.

"Will we buy juice?"
asked Mr. Jones.

Mrs. Jones looked down
at the list and smiled.
"The only thing on
this list is cheese!"
she said, laughing.

Shopping List
cheese
chocolates
raspberries
ice cream
nuts
juice